Love Rises

How to Move From Rock Bottom to Living a Courageously Confident Life

Leslie Sepe

With Gratitude:

Thank you to my beautiful daughters for the love and support you always extend to me. You both are the wind beneath my wings. Thank you to my mom for living a life of forgiveness and unconditional love. Thank you to all the family, friends, co-workers and mentors who have helped me to move forward in life. Thank you to my pastors for teaching me the value of God's word. When the chips were down in my life, you placed hope in my heart. A special thank you to my nephew who lived a life of strength and courage despite his lifelong battle with asthma.

© 2021 Leslie Therese Sepe

All rights reserved. No part of this publication may be reproduced, stored in a retrieval system, stored in a database and / or published in any form or by any means, electronic, mechanical, photocopying, recording or otherwise, without the prior written permission of the publisher.

All permission requests are to be directed via e-mail to Leslie@lesliesepeconsulting.com with the subject line of "Attention: Permissions Coordinator".

First Edition - April 2021

Book design, front cover and illustrations by Leslie Sepe

ISBN: 978-0-578-88953-5 (For Paperback)
ISBN: 978-0-578-88954-2 (For E-book)

Table of Contents

INTRODUCTION: 11

Chapter 1:
Wrestling With Rock Bottom 13

Chapter 2:
Finding a Place of Refuge 19

Chapter 3:
A New Beginning 22

Chapter 4:
The Struggle Is Real 32

Chapter 5:
Opening Myself Up to New Possibilities 39

Chapter 6:
The Gift of Forgiveness 45

Chapter 7:
Embracing a New Journey 50

Chapter 8:
Humility Is Your Friend 60

Chapter 9:
Living Your Best Life With Gratitude: 69

INTRODUCTION:

Life has a way of taking us on a journey filled with all sorts of experiences that cause us to carry a variety of feelings and emotions along for the ride. We may find ourselves experiencing joy-filled events such as the birth of a child, the celebration of marriage, graduating from an educational institution, success in our careers and so on.

Other times, we may find that life throws us an unexpected curveball. We may have the rug pulled out from under us by experiences we find ourselves in the midst of that we never planned for or would have imagined would take place in our lives.

What do we do when the latter becomes a reality? What do you do when you find yourself in a position that is not at all favorable, when the chips are down and you are experiencing a low point in your life? What do you do when you are feeling defeated or devastated by life's events and possibly hitting rock bottom?

Where do we turn? What do we do? How do we react? Who is to blame? We sometimes ask ourselves "why me?"

My desire to write this book came from a personal experience when, for a period of time in my life, all the chips were down. I had hit rock bottom from a divorce and the tide of life was flowing against me. I chose to not make this period of my life my destiny.

Introduction

It is my hope that through the steps I have taken to turn my life around as I share in this book, you too will choose to step into a pathway of healing, forgiveness, abundance, prosperity, courage and all richness of life God has waiting for you to claim.

Chapter 1: Wrestling With Rock Bottom

The door slammed shut, and for the first time in years, I was all alone.

The feeling of anguish and pain engulfed my heart.

This should have been a night where we, as a family, celebrated the high school graduation of our oldest daughter.

Sitting on the foyer stairs, I watched my daughters leave with their suitcases to go to their dad's townhome. I was lost in despair and wondered to myself how this could be. I wanted to open the door and shout to them to come back. But, I refrained from doing so. I didn't want to upset my children. Their hearts were already hurting, as they felt torn between their parents' marital conflict.

Turning the lights off, I retreated to my master bedroom. I felt lost in my own home. It was all too quiet. I desperately wanted my family with me. Feelings of anger and desperation filled my heart, and I was left to my own thoughts. Why did my ex-husband get to have the girls the night our oldest daughter graduated from high school? I am the parent who spent countless hours and years homeschooling our daughter. It just didn't seem fair. I felt cheated.

Heartbroken, I laid in bed, my gut wrenched with pain. Sleep was impossible. In the hope of being consoled, I decided to journal and put pen to paper expressing my pain. I begged for God's mercy to get me through the night. Exhaustion set in and I turned out the lights.

Sleep did not restore my hurting soul. It would take years for my heartache, guilt, anger and shame to be lifted.

Lost and Confused
Two lives intertwined and destined to accomplish so much. The world was our oyster. We had a wedding day that was fully celebrated on the foundation of "'til death do us part" and lavishness that was fit for a princess. Our professional careers were on the rise. We built a beautiful custom home as our abode, and we were eager to create a home filled with special memories.

The birth of our daughters brought such joy into our lives and entwined our hearts even deeper. The sound of their laughter and the pitter-patter of their little feet echoed throughout the halls.

Entertaining family and friends for holiday celebrations and special occasions was fun and a bonding experience for us. We worked hard together to make our home warm and welcoming. We shared a strong Christian faith that provided strength and hope as we encountered the daily grind and difficulties of life.

A strong work ethic existed in both of us. We were not afraid to roll up our sleeves and take on the challenges of life. He worked hard to provide for our family, and I worked hard at creating a loving home.

We cherished our daughters and were committed to providing the best parenting we knew how. As the years passed, homeschooling became the way of educating our children. I relished in the opportunity to teach my daughters at home and spend so much time with them. Their education was filled with diverse learning opportunities and they thrived in all areas of their lives. We were proud parents.

Life would prove to be not always easy, and at times we were challenged to our tipping point.

My ex-husband's strong ties to a family culture in which pleasing the parents is a high priority, suffocated and angered me over time. That situation, coupled with him working in his family's business, would prove to be the perfect recipe for bringing me to the breaking point, causing me to want out of our marriage.

We did seek marital counseling, but a resolution and agreement could not be found. I would not be controlled and ruled by his expectations. I sought a pathway out, and it came through divorce.

Twenty-three years of marriage was dissolved with the stroke of a pen as we signed the divorce documents.

Walking out of the courthouse, I was in a state of disbelief. I felt so small in a world that had now become so big. I was alone. I was afraid. I was in disbelief. Despite the fact I filed for divorce, the emotional pain ran deep and wide. My now-former husband would no longer walk beside me as my friend, lover, supporter and encourager.

He would now take on the role of my ex-husband. He would be a foe and not a friend. His friendship, advice, help, care and concern were expunged from my life. How does one begin to step into a future that was never planned for?

Severed Relationships

The loss would be more than I bargained for. My daughters would take the brunt of the blow. My heart was wrought with pain as I watched the turmoil take its toll. Sorrow, anger and deep pain would now become the emotional friends of my daughters. I felt I had failed as their mom. I did not model all my talk of "marriage for life". I feared they would never forgive me. I cherished our mother and daughter relationship and their love for me. I was gravely afraid that I would lose their respect and that they would no longer want to spend time with me in favor of their father.

Adding more pain to my already-existing pain, some of my friends became distant and judged me for seeking a divorce. They only saw the outside of my marriage. They saw me as a friend who "had it all". Without want, I did have the privilege to stay home and homeschool my daughters, live in a large and beautiful custom-built home with a heated built-in swimming pool. We took wonderful vacations, I drove a luxury car, owned expensive jewelry and a fur coat. I lived a life void of material wants. Although I did enjoy the luxuries, they are not who I am at my core. I can pitch and sleep in a tent and live in a palace feeling content in either situation.

I remember one specific day like it was yesterday. I ventured out to attend a birthday party for a very dear, life-long friend. No sooner did I arrive at the party than I was greeted by another friend who decided to attack me verbally and tell me to stop playing the victim. These words cut me to the core, like a knife slicing through an apple. This accusation was so off course. I wondered how such a loving friend could turn on me. I was distraught and deeply hurt. Fortunately, months later, my friend did apologize for her words and behavior. She was acting out of fear. I chose to let love rise, and I immediately and lovingly forgave her.

It was not long after I got divorced that I would return to what was once my home to pick up a few belongings. When I entered the house where I no longer lived, I found two of my friends who happen to be in the home improvement business in my kitchen. They were tearing it apart because my ex was embarking on remodeling the kitchen. It cut me to the core. My heart was being torn apart — so was what had once been the place that was the heart of our home, where so many wonderful family dinners took place.

I found that certain people were just plain oblivious to my pain and my children's pain. As I retreated to the front door, my friend came out to join me to offer me her support and apologize for turning her back on me. I immediately and lovingly forgave her. The construction project went forward. My ex-husband would have a new and gorgeous kitchen, regardless of how it made me feel.

Thankfully, the number of friends who had turned against me for a short time was fewer than I can count on one hand. Because I chose to let love rise, today those relationships are restored.

Emotional and Spiritual Pain

Wrought with emotional despair, I would endure a strike against my physical and spiritual wellbeing. I blamed myself for the breakdown of my marriage. I was plagued with guilt. As a woman of faith, I felt unworthy of God's love. Feelings are emotions that cannot be trusted. I made an agreement with a lie. I lived in a state of shame and failure, and living in this position soon made my health spiral downward. I soon begin to experience abdominal pain and bloating coupled with anxiety, leaving me physically compromised. I became thin and physically frail; my strong and healthy physique was no longer recognizable.

Forgive Yourself

Life's events take place, and at times our behaviors, actions or experiences leave us feeling pain, anguish, guilt and shame. We may feel we were partly responsible for the chain of events. You may even blame yourself. When we find ourselves in such a situation forgiveness toward oneself is important to begin the recovery process from divorce. The process of forgiving yourself will set the foundation to lift the burden of shame and guilt.

The practice of daily journaling allows you to put your thoughts on paper providing a pathway to expunge ill feelings. Writing words of affirmation in your journal or speaking them out loud to yourself provides you with an opportunity to express love and appreciation toward yourself.

The healing process from divorce takes time, and we do not need to go it alone. Seeking emotional support will give you a community of people to help you along the road to healing. If you have children, make them a priority in your life. They, too, need help along the way to healing.

Most importantly, seek the advice of a doctor if necessary.

Chapter 2: Finding a Place of Refuge

I Am Forgiven
Where do I turn? Deep in my heart, I knew running toward the Lord was my best strategy for recovery and healing. I know where my help comes from. Because I had asked for the divorce, I decided I would be the one to leave our home church, where we had attended for so many years with our daughters. Leaving many long-term, faithful and loving relationships was not easy. Embarking on finding a new church was frightening for me. How would I be welcomed? Would I make new friends easily? I showed up like a lost and hurting puppy at the door of The Harbor Church, and was welcomed and embraced immediately with love and kindness.

"Come to me all who are weary and heavy laden and I will give you rest"
(Matthew 11:28)

Healing Through Honesty
Seeking emotional, physical and spiritual healing, I would soon discover that blame was not the name of the game. Consistently attending church services, prayer meetings and bible studies as well as listening to worship music, would aid in my healing. God would be so tender as I was led to look inward and evaluate my behavior that contributed to my divorce. With scripture as my guide, God lovingly revealed to

me where I was not at my best. Lack of forgiveness, anger and having to be right, did not serve me well. Honesty is the best policy, even toward yourself. Guilt and shame melted away.

> "And the truth shall set you free"
> **(John 8:32)**

Grace, Mercy and Peace

I received unconditional love from Christ. Grace, mercy and peace are mine for the taking. Growing deeper in my walk with the Lord, He continued to reveal to me His love for me as I embraced His redemptive power. Christ pulled me from the dark pit of divorce leading to feelings of brokenness, shame and guilt. God is not a God of condemnation. God has proven that He is too faithful to fail me. He keeps me in the valley and hides me from the rain. He is my rock, my shield and my refuge in whom I take shelter.

> "For I know the plans that I have for you," declares the Lord, "plans for welfare and not for calamity to give you a future and a hope. **(Jeremiah 29:11)**

Reflect and Evaluate

Divorce brings change. Sometimes that change can leave you feeling lost and alone. Life becomes different leaving you to question how will I heal? What are my next steps? Where do I turn?

Seek God and receive unconditional love, mercy and grace. God offers a love that goes deep to heal and restore the wounds of our heart. Love, mercy and grace are ours for the taking, restoring our mind, body and spirit. God wants us to come to Him with our burdens so He can give us rest.

Having a courageous spirit to make an inward reflection will serve you well toward your journey of healing. Take time to reflect and evaluate your actions and behaviors that are displayed in your relationships. Ask God where you need to change.

It is not an easy process to embark upon, but it is one that will help you discover character traits and behaviors that do not serve you or your relationships in a positive light. Embrace the truth about yourself and make changes where necessary.

Chapter 3:
A New Beginning

Loss of the Things You Love
Who will take what? We listed our assets and split what we owned. Oh, what a horrible process to go through. All the years of hard work to make our house a home was being dismantled in a tug of war.

Words cannot express the excruciating emotional pain of packing my belongings to leave a home I had occupied for 23 years. There were so many beautiful memories. Packing pictures of my daughters, I reflected on the special memories we shared together that were now wrapped and placed in a box to be stored away.

My wedding portrait had been taken down from the wall in the center hall.

I remember vividly the day one of my friends came to help me pack my china. Oh, how I loved its pattern of subtle beauty. We talked about how family and friends would gather at my dining room table for the holidays and special occasions. We reminisced about the laughter, the conversations that took place and how the table was beautifully appointed.

Each piece was wrapped and packed away. I could not believe what was happening. My friend encouraged me with her kind words of support. She was no stranger to life's difficulties. She carefully wrapped each piece of china with great care, ensuring me she was an expert at packing fragile items. I am forever grateful for her consideration and faithful friendship.

As the boxes piled high, the house became more like a shell of possessions. It was becoming more of a reality that I would be leaving the place I had called home. To help manage my emotions, I would walk into each room daily and take a mental picture of what it looked like and I would bring to memory the special moments that each room held. I didn't want to let go of the good that had happened there. I found comfort in the memories of tucking my children to bed and the nightly ritual of bedtime stories. I recalled with happiness, my daughters playing with their Barbie dolls lined up on the staircase and the hallway upstairs, the forts they would make on the upstairs foyer and playing with their dolls.

The memories of the fun we had splashing in the pool and playing Marco Polo and the echoing of their laughter still clung in the air.

Stepping into my youngest daughter's room, which served as the nursery for both of my children, the memories of when they were infants and recalling the nightly ritual of holding and signing to them as the sound of my voice lulled them to sleep came flooding back to me. It was a time I remember as so precious and sweet.

There were cookouts, birthday parties, prom parties, sitting up late and watching the shooting stars. Fifteen years of homeschooling memories in our home. There were so many wonderful heartwarming events to cherish.

Packing each belonging brought deep regret and sorrow

over a failed marriage.

After weeks of packing, the day came when the moving trucks pulled up in the driveway. I did not want this day to come, but come it did. Within a few hours, all my possessions had been loaded onto the truck. I took one last look behind me as I closed the front door to what had been my home for 23 years.

My ex-husband changed the locks immediately, solidifying the mark that I no longer had a claim to what once was my home.

Not only would the loss of my home plague my heart with emptiness, but the loss of friends with whom we had spent so much time with raising our children was difficult, too. It still baffles me today that good friends could abandon me because of divorce. The phone would not ring for me to find a friendly voice on the other end asking how my children and I were doing. There was nothing — just silence. It was something that I had to learn to live with and come to terms with to be free from disappointment and regret.

I chose to let love rise and extend the gift of forgiveness.

Making New Connections
Life would be different. Most of my friends were married and spent their free time with their husbands. Time alone was now the norm. My oldest daughter was off to college and my youngest daughter was going back and forth between my home and her dad's.

How would I fill my time? My new place of worship would provide the opportunity for me to make new friends. The church is located close to the local university, so it attracted many international graduate-level college students. It would prove to be a great asset for making new connections.

The international students needed help getting settled in their new surroundings in the United States. I was ready and willing to help through my church's outreach ministry.

Weekly, we met on Thursday evenings on the college campus to have a light dinner, play games and offer a place for the students to make new friends outside the classroom setting.

Each week students from various counties would host a dinner and cook foods from their homeland. We all enjoyed foods from Brazil, India, Sri Lanka, Africa and Iran. The students shared information about their homelands so we could learn more about them and their individual cultures. I found all of this so interesting and lots of fun. I felt like I was traveling the world without having to get on an airplane.

I developed close relationships with some of the students and they soon felt more like my children than friends. I would take them for dinner to various restaurants, celebrate holidays at my home, shop and sight-see in Boston. One particular trip I hold dear to my heart is a road trip a small group of us took to Washington, D.C. to attend a conference. We had so much fun visiting various museums and celebrating New Year's Eve together.

Having met so many students from different parts of the world gave me a beautiful perspective that we share common desires. We all want to be loved, have dreams and look to seek meaningful relationships. Life's challenges know no geographic or cultural boundary. Hope and love live in all our hearts.

I made a conscious effort to take advantage of any and all opportunities that were presented to me to make new friends. Being open and curious would prove to be an asset to me. Knowing that developing a new community of support would be extremely important to my emotional well being.

I ventured out and joined BNI (Business Networking International). It is an international business organization with local chapters having no more than 40 members within each group, and no two members can represent the same type of business. I held a spot for my esthetics business, Radiance by Leslie.

It proved to be a great way to increase my client base as well as making many new professional contacts. Throughout the years, I have utilized many of the BNI member services and received excellent service. I had trusted business professionals I could turn to and recommend for business needs.

Adjusting Emotionally
The ability to be emotionally intelligent would allow me to navigate the emotional ups and downs of living as a divorced single mom with success. I soon recognized how quickly I could be self-aware of my emotions, identify them and respond in a healthy manner, which would prove to be the key to experiencing vibrant emotional health.

Journaling would be a way for me to release emotional tension and stress. Before bed or sometimes in the morning, I would make it a priority to journal about what was in my heart. I could immediately feel the stress being released as I put pen to paper. I wrote out my feelings as well as my prayer requests.

Here are a few of the journal entries that I wrote during this season. I hope you'll find them useful as you walk through your own journey of healing.

Journal entry Friday, June 11, 2015

*Father God Almighty,
Thank you for the privilege of knowing you. Lord, I ask you to help me cope, deal and forgive my ex-husband for his thoughtless acts against me. Lord you are my God and King. I praise you, praise you, praise you. I ask you to help me. Help me. Help me.
Please watch over my daughters. Lord, this life can be so hard. Thank you Lord. Thank you.*

Journal entry Sunday, June 18, 2016

*Dear Lord Father God,
Praise your holy name. Thank you for the privilege to come before you and lift my requests to you. Father, my desire is to please you. My desire is to be blessed by you. Lord, you know right now I am afraid, I am overwhelmed with the financial decisions I have before me. Lord, please guide me. Father please bless me.*

Journal entry June 16, 2017

Thank you. Thank you. Thank you. Lord you have been gracious to me. Lord you love me. Lord you have forgiven me. Lord I am your Special Lady. Father may I never take for granted the many provisions and blessings that you have helped me with. Lord, I have learned to say "thank you" for the divorce. Lord, it has helped me to discover who I am, the past difficulties of my childhood and how these experiences formulated my sensitivities, my way of thinking and why I do what I do, say what I say, and feel what I feel.

Jesus, I am feeling lonely. Jesus, I am feeling tired. Lord, I am feeling this life is so hard. Lord, I know it is through your strength that I will be sustained.

Lord, help me to honor you in the way I spend my money. Help me to sacrifice according to your will for my life. Jesus, you are my king, my refuge, my stronghold, my Jahova Raffa (my healer), my sustainer, my friend, my secure foundation.

Praise you my Lord and King. Father, I beg of your mercies, grace, provisions, forgiveness on behalf of my daughters and

ex-husband. Lord, you know what is going on in their lives. You know where the kingdom of darkness is attacking. I beg of your intercession on their behalf. Jesus, praise you, praise you, praise you.

Help me, Lord, to have a very successful day of selling at my job. Help me to learn all I need to learn with the computer and the processing of paperwork. Praise you Jesus. Praise you.

=== end journal entries ===

The consistent habit of journaling would prove not only to help me heal emotionally, but my journal entries would provide an opportunity for me to track my progress of emotional healing through the years.

In addition to journaling, long walks became a way for me to process my emotions. For years I have walked in my favorite wildlife refuge by the sea. The ocean provided not only a beautiful view but the fresh salty air, sunshine and creatures of nature helped to release stress. The expanse of the ocean reminded me of the expanse of the power of God.

Year after year I have sought refuge in my favorite wildlife sanctuary. It was my special place to seek the face of God. I walked alone along the long loop set on the ocean side and had conversations with God, during which I poured my heart out. I would climb to the highest rock peak and lift my hands up to the sky making my requests known. I believe strongly in the power of prayer and waited patiently for my answers.

Persistence and patience was the name of the game. I walked by faith and not by sight. Many of my prayers have been answered in God's time. One answered prayer was writing a book to encourage others in the power of God's redemption. No matter how deep and dark the pit may be that we need rescuing from when we seek the help from God, He is sure to extend a helping hand.

Let Go of the Past and Embrace the New
The process of letting go of things you love especially due to a divorce is emotionally painful. Most often divorce causes the loss of material possessions and also the dynamics of some relationships are altered. Moving forward from such loss can be challenging and overwhelming.

Embracing the opportunity to build a new community of friends and connections can be fun and exciting. There are many possibilities available offering exposure to new experiences. Don't wait or hesitate; you never know who you will meet or what doors will open to you. Enjoy the process and in time you will be making new friends and creating new memories.

Putting pen to paper through the process of journaling helps to process emotions and increase self awareness. "When we translate an experience into language we essentially make the experience graspable. And in doing so, you free yourself from mentally being tangled in traumas. Journaling will also provide a way, a roadmap so to speak, for you to track your progress of emotional recovery and healing.

Prayer is a gift to be cherished and honored. Prayer is an opportunity for us to talk with God, to seek direction and receive direction in our life. We do not have to be kneeling to pray we can talk with God wherever we are and whatever we are doing. As we commit ourselves to a consistent prayer life things are revealed to us and we can achieve a lot in our life as God gives us direction. We can seek God through prayer for emotional, physical and spiritual healing.

Chapter 4:
The Struggle Is Real

Building New Skills

When my first daughter was born, I had decided I did not want to go back to work in my sales position in corporate America. I wanted to stay home and raise my daughter. Eventually, I would take on the role not only as a parent, but the role of a homeschooling teacher. I was thrilled to homeschool my two daughters, and the journey lasted 15 years.

When I got divorced and went back into the workforce, I found myself at a disadvantage. The business environment had changed drastically. I was not computer literate, which proved to be a challenge.

To gain work experience, I took on various temp jobs that would put a few dollars in my pocket. But, they did not build the skills I needed, nor did they help me meet my financial obligations. Some of the jobs were interesting. I had the opportunity to work at "The Elms Mansion" in Newport, RI as a tour guide aide. This three-week employment opportunity provided me with lots of knowledge of what Newport was like during the Gilded Age. I love history and the preservation of old buildings, so I was in my happy place.

At times, the number of visitors to the mansion was low, which provided me the opportunity to watch over the conservatory. I would sit on a wooden bench that was situated in the corner of the room and take some quiet reflective time. I was in my glory. I would take this time to thank God for all the abundances that were combining into my life.

I wanted to be sure I maintained a grateful heart attitude.

A Wake-Up Call
The worst temp job I had was a month-long position at a non-profit organization that helped moms who were disadvantaged and needed assistance. Although I loved the organization's mission to help women and their children, the work was physically demanding and demeaning.

My first task was to work in a run-down warehouse filled with used furnishings that were old and broken. One room that was located way back in the warehouse was piled high with boxes of clothes that had been donated. The room was extremely unorganized and was not heated (mind you, it was December in New England). I was promised the heat would be turned on, however it never happened. Although I was bundled up in winter attire every day, I still was frozen to my bones. I had the responsibility of organizing the clothing to get it ready to give to the families in need. My co-worker and I finished the job successfully, and in record time.

I was then moved to a larger, empty, and thankfully heated, warehouse with an open space where we would collect and place the donated bags of toys for the Christmas season. It was my and my co-worker's responsibility to section off the warehouse floor numerically and alphabetically with tape so we could have an organized system to receive and give away the bags of donations when the social workers came to pick them up.

I remember the day I had to section off the floor with tape like it was yesterday. I was kneeling on the cement floor on my hands and knees. This position was physically painful. I couldn't help but wonder why God was letting this happen to me after I had homeschooled my children and supported my ex-husband while he was building his successful business. I had a college education and ended up working in a warehouse, kneeling on a cement floor. It wasn't fair.

My financial challenges made recovering from the divorce that much harder. Paying the bills on time and in full was becoming more and more difficult. I frequently wondered where I could go and what I could do to bring me financial stability.

There were days when my cupboards were bare and buying food to fill my empty belly was a real challenge. I did not want to burden my family, so they did not know how desperate my financial situation had become. I had not learned how to totally put aside my pride.

I was in a desperate place. Sitting in my car by the ocean one afternoon and feeling overwhelmed, scared and crying, I reached out to a friend to explain my situation, and she referred me to her company to seek employment.

Thankfully, this referral worked out and I was hired for a full-time position as an inside sales rep for one of the largest companies in the hotel industry. I was hired in the call center to book hotel rooms. Working with a tenacious spirit, I proved myself skilled in sales, and within nine months I had received two promotions.

I ended up working on the corporate side of the business in group sales — a position coveted by many employees.

I was immediately given a project that enabled me to work

with hotels across the nation to expand a reward program for the corporate side of the hotels. Drawing on skills I had developed years ago while working in the technology industry selling small local area networks to K-12 academic institutions, I was able to achieve the goals set before me. My manager recognized my strong work ethic, sales skill ability and celebrated my achievements of reaching corporate sales goals.

Proving the strength of my sales skills, I was given a second project of helping the company transition through a corporate sales merge. Although this project did not involve sales, the tasks I was responsible for implementing allowed me to gain experience in project management.

My future was beginning to look bright.

Listening to Your Inner Voice
I was making progress in building a resume, but I was still not making enough money to make ends meet. Seeking to improve my situation, I continued to look for opportunities that would increase my annual income. Going against my better judgement, I took a job with a company as an office manager because it promised growth within the company. I was hesitant to take the job because I really like sales and this job was a "desk job" that didn't offer the daily tasks or skill set I really enjoy or excel at.

Within two days at the job, I wondered what I had gotten myself into. This job was not me, and the company was not great to work for. Training was non-existent, the office staff was unfriendly and my direct manager had no time or desire to train me. I was left to fend for myself.

One week later I was fired from the job. I jumped for joy and was so thankful!!!! No more abuse. I did not have to go to work at a job that did not position me to excel in my strength of sales. I was so happy and made the decision to always listen to my "inner voice" to guide me along the path of life.

I am thankful for the nudging of the Holy Spirit in my life, or as some would say, listening to your intuition. As I traveled the road to recovery and healing from my divorce the Lord would be ever so gracious to lead me to take action to further my journey of healing.

Listening to the whispering of the Holy Spirit, I found myself driving over to my ex-husband's home one Easter Sunday. My ex-husband and children were visiting family out of state, so I knew no one would be home.

With the feeling of butterflies in my stomach, I drove up the long driveway and parked my car in front of the middle garage door. I got out of the car and proceeded to walk laps around the house remembering the many beautiful events that happened in what was once our family home. I recalled these special experiences. With my hands and voice lifted, I thanked God for the privilege to come back to this house and to express a " prayer of thankfulness". It was my opportunity for closure and healing.

I didn't care if the neighbors saw me. I had no problem sharing with my ex what God had called me to do. God was ordering my steps of healing.

I got in my car and drove down the long driveway and headed back to my apartment. However, the Holy Spirit tugged at my heart again. I was not finished. I felt led to turn the car around and go back to walk three more laps around the house. I thought that I must be crazy, but still knew it was best for me to take action as the nudge was presented.

I headed back to my ex-husband's house, parked the car again in the same place as before, got out and proceeded to walk three more laps around his house. This time with more fervent vocal prayer with my arms lifted up.

It was an experience of completion. I could reset my heart and soul. I felt closure had occurred and I am forever grateful for this opportunity. Saying "yes" and having the courage to go forth brought a sustaining joy and peace to my heart.

I thank the Lord for the power of the Holy Spirit and God's mercy and grace extended toward me. Say "yes" to the smallest and largest whispers from the Holy Spirit. A gift that is available to all of us.

You Can Press On
The drive to push on to find a job that would pay me enough to support myself was underway once again. One of my favorite scripture verses "Let us not grow weary or become discouraged in doing good, for at the proper time we will reap, if we do not give in" (**Galatians 6:9**) encourages me to find strength when the going gets tough. Years of rebuilding my resume at times was overwhelming.

Giving up was not an option. I was determined to be successful. I will press on physically and emotionally, and without ceasing.

Free to look for another job, I landed a sales position in the furniture industry where I would experience success. This was not my last job, but it paved the way for me to gain sales experience that would prove to move me forward in my sales career. Step by step, I was progressing onward and making a concerted effort to be the best employee I could be.

My efforts would bring forth fruit. My annual income was moving in the right direction.

Press On, Move Forward and Believe in Yourself
Pressing on and moving forward from divore can be met with obstacles for various reasons. Financial stress and burdens are often the norm rather than the exception. Taking steps to building a strong and stable financial portfolio requires you to move forward with a tenacious and preserving spirit.

To build new skills or to seek employment, temporary job agencies can provide a way for you to build your resume. You have exposure to many different companies offering a wide variety of training opportunities. With each new employment position, your skills will gradually begin to improve leading to the possibility of your dream job. Be sure to embark on employment opportunities that build on your strengths.

The leading of the Holy Spirit is a powerful resource in our life. As we pay attention to the leading of the Holy Spirit we will be guided to take steps unique to our life. Step out in faith. God knows what is best for us.

There is no quick fix to moving forward and rebuilding your life. Step after step takes courage. Press on and move forward believing one day you will receive what you have been seeking to achieve. Believe in yourself and do not give up.

Chapter 5: Opening Myself Up to New Possibilities

The Power of Dreaming

I attended a multi-level marketing convention, for which the crowd exceeded 10,000 people. The guest speaker immediately drew me in as he sat at the edge of the stage with his feet dangling over the edge. He told us his story of his father's tremendous favorable impact on his life. He spoke with deep love from his heart, and it radiated out to the audience. This was the first time I had heard John C. Maxwell speak. I had no idea that he is a best-selling author and speaker on the topic of leadership and personal development.

The burning desire to propel my life forward would not rest. Wanting to achieve my dreams, I embarked on a quest to learn more about the Maxwell organization. I emailed my request for information, and I soon received a call from one of the program coordinators.

I sat on my bed one evening speaking to the program coordinator about the details of becoming a Maxwell certified speaker, trainer and life coach. As we discussed the details, I was extremely excited at the thought of going forward with the program.

We discussed the time commitment it would take, which did not pose a roadblock for me joining the program. However, the financial commitment for this program was a big nut to swallow. I would have to take a few thousand dollars out of my 401K just for the entry-level commitment, and I already had withdrawn plenty of money to make ends meet. It was so scary for me because at this time I was only working part-time in my esthetics business and profits were slim.

Taking inventory of where I was in life and the benefits the program provided, I decided to say "yes" to improving myself and embarking on my personal development journey, believing that I am worth the investment!!!

The journey began with a 90-day immersion program with two of the most fabulous trainers from the Maxwell certification program. They were filled with wit and energy, making a perfect team to help me begin the journey of implementing personal growth and leadership principles into my life daily. They believed in me, which gave me the strength and confidence to believe in myself. They helped me and encouraged me. Success was mine for the taking.

During the immersion program, I was given an assignment to help me learn the importance of writing down my dreams. What was I deeply longing to have, be or do in my life? I wrote about a dream home I hope to own in the future. I was advised to write in specific detail what the home would look like. Every minute detail had to be described.

As I described my dream home to my mentors, it helped me to visualize owning a dream home and not just thinking or just speaking about it. The combination of thinking, speaking and writing down my dream required my full brain to go to work. An amplified effect occurred and helped my dream become a reality.

I have practiced this exercise for many of my dreams as they relate to various realms in my life such as my health, relationships, finances and business. I have set a practice to revisit what I have written down every few months or so and add more specific details as they arise.

I was thirsty for knowledge on the topic of leadership and began a seven-year journey of studying and reading books on leadership that I worked on consistently. I found encouragement from the experts. They provided hope for me. If they could overcome challenges in life by mastering the art of leadership so could I.

Time Spent Alone
I believed that I needed time alone to heal and to work on discovering where I needed to personally grow and develop. I did not want to go from one relationship to another and bring unhealed emotions and personal baggage into a new relationship. Also, I was extremely discerning of who I would introduce to my daughters.

As I look back at my life during this period of intentional time alone, it would prove to be a time of so many blessings for me personally.

I was always available to my daughters, who were in college at this point. Whenever they needed to talk with me, I was available to answer their calls. We would share great conversations, and I was thankful I was home to take their phone calls, give advice and offer encouragement to them. I will never regret these moments, and I cherish them in my heart to this day. I wanted my daughters to know that I am here for them always and they are my most cherished priority in life.

I never wanted to waste time dating around (you may feel differently, and that is perfectly fine). and as of today it has been eight years that I have been single and happy.

Many people were surprised that I did not date and several friends began to ask me why I didn't go on dating sites. My answer was simply that I don't want to go looking. I have watched many of my friends go through so many dates, waste time, get disappointed and have horrible experiences only to come up empty. Simply put, the dating sites are just not for me and I am happy with my decision.

You attract who you are. Period. End of story. I knew I needed healing and to make changes within myself if I wanted to avoid another failed marriage. The focus needed to be on becoming the best version of myself.

Faithfully, for seven years, on Saturday nights, I would pack up my favorite books, bible and journal and sit by the ocean reading, writing and praying. The sunsets were beautiful and I did not feel alone. I put my dreams down on paper and made plans of implementation to make them a reality. I prayed to God for myself, my ex-husband, daughters, family, friends, co-workers, etc. It was a sweet sweet time in my life and I will cherish the memories in my heart forever.

Yes, there were moments when I would ask God how long he planned on having me spend time alone before He brought the man of my dreams into my life. The answer was that I needed to be patient. I trust and know God's timing is always perfect. My life coach always reminds me that God is preparing the man to be equipped to offer his best to you. I always respond with a chuckle, and I certainly agree.

"For I have learned to be content in whatever circumstances I am"
(**Philippians 4:11**)

Beginning to Thrive

Life was becoming a bit brighter. Peace filled my heart more and more throughout the days. New friends entered my life. Employment opportunities continued to come my way. We were all healing from the divorce.

I had taken the opportunity to travel on business trips and make lots of fun memories with friends and business associates.

I traveled to Texas, Florida, New York City, Los Angeles, San Francisco, Kentucky and Wisconsin on business. My sales profession allowed me to develop relationships with associates from around the country. Learning was made fun by the various manufacturers. I was spoiled by a trip to Churchill Downs, sunset cruises and private dinner parties prepared by the most talented chefs, and the dinner tables were elaborately set.

One of the most fun business trips I took was to Southern California. I flew in a bit early and walked to a nearby hotel to have lunch and sit by the pool. While I was relaxing and enjoying myself, a parade of incredibly strong, athletically-built men walked by my table. It did not take me long to get up the courage to stop one young man and ask if they were football players. Sure enough, the Los Angeles Chargers football team was staying at the hotel during a preseason practice.

What's a girl to do? I began a two-day mission to get as many pictures taken with the different football players and get their autographs. I had so much fun. I sent pictures to my co-workers and daughters to share the exciting news. My oldest daughter loves football, so I was sure to collect a few autographs.

When opportunity presents itself, one must be ready to take action!!

Life is what you make of it. Don't be shy. Take a chance and see where life brings you.

Dreaming, Reflecting and Taking Action
What do you really want in life? Our dreams often speak to us about things we long for or are discontent with. Take the time to reflect and tune into the signals life is presenting to you. Begin the process of writing down your dreams in very specific detail. Revisit what you have written often and revise when necessary.

Time alone is a beautiful and precious gift you can give to yourself. Intentionally carve out time just for yourself. It is a time to be used for prayer, self reflection, rest, healing, reading or goal setting. Time alone gives you space to reflect and get in tune with yourself to figure out what you and you alone want out of life. You get to decide how much time you need to take alone based on your unique needs.

Embrace the power of "yes" and take action on opportunities that are presented to you. You alone are responsible for the direction of your life. Opportunities come and go and if we do not take action when we have the chance the opportunity is sure to pass us by.

Chapter 6: The Gift of Forgiveness

Freedom to Forgive Yourself
   Sometimes it is more difficult to forgive yourself than it is to forgive others. For years I blamed myself for a failed marriage because I asked for the divorce. So many times I would feel a deep pang of guilt and pain in my stomach because my family was broken up.

   I remember the day my ex-husband and two daughters sat in the family counselor's office like it was yesterday. My daughters sat close together opposite from me on a couch. My oldest daughter took the position of protector of her younger sister and offered her emotional support and courage.

   When my husband uttered that he and I were getting a divorce, my youngest daughter burst into tears and expressed deep sadness because she thought that she was losing her family. The remembrance of the anguish on her face made my heart very heavy for years. It was extremely difficult to see my daughters in such distress.

   One particular evening, my daughter returned home for a visit during her first semester of her freshman year at college. As we sat on her bed catching up on life's events, she cried because she was the only one of her college friends who had parents who are divorced. It broke my heart.

Moments like this made me feel that I was selfish to have gotten a divorce and should have stayed married. My relationship with my daughters was always healthy, and we shared a close bond as mother and daughters. I had the privilege of spending extensive hours of time with them because I homeschooled them. That time together helped us to create a special bond. I wanted to be sure their love and respect for me would always remain.

I made sure I took the time to speak to each daughter individually to apologize and ask for their forgiveness for the divorce and take responsibility for where I thought I failed in my marriage. We could not erase what had happened, but I wanted my daughters to know that I was truly sorry that their dad and I were no longer together in marriage.

I was sorry for their pain. We were all experiencing pain, including their dad.

Having the courage to be vulnerable with my daughters allowed our relationship to begin to heal. I also began to heal and extend love to myself. Love would lay the foundation of transformation from shame and guilt to embracing a new found respect and love I held for myself.

Forgiving yourself is one of the best gifts you can extend to yourself.

Extending the Olive Branch
After my divorce, there were years of struggle with my ex-husband. He did not have a forgiving heart and blamed me for breaking up our family. My desire was to have our daughters experience peace when they were spending time together with their now-divorced parents.

I wanted to be a uniting force as much as possible between a divorced couple.

Spending much time in prayer and journaling made me sensitive to the leading of the Holy Spirit. God laid on my heart a message to send a note to my ex-husband's parents to let them know I was sorry for the hurt they had experienced because of the divorce and ask for their forgiveness.

I did not jump on this nudging by God so quickly. Actually, I wondered if that was what He really wanted me to do. Because my desire was for healing and harmony, after several months I wrote the note and sent the card. Neither my ex-husband nor his parents ever acknowledged receiving the note.

God also spoke to my heart and told me to ask my ex-husband to forgive me, and I did so without hesitation.

I know in my heart that I did what I was called to do and stepped out in great vulnerability and courage. I took action in faith knowing God would honor my faithfulness.

Prayer was a big factor in extending love to my ex-husband. For years, when I prayed with my daughters, I made sure I would lift their father in prayer and ask for blessings upon his life in all areas. I desired that my ex-husband be blessed not only for himself, but because my daughters would be at peace knowing their father was experiencing God's blessings.

Pressing on When Your Ex Cannot Forgive

Verbal expression of forgiveness is different from a true acceptance and extension of forgiveness in your heart. When we offer forgiveness from the depths of our heart and soul to someone who has hurt us, offended us or wronged us, the act of kindness is often a by-product.

Sometimes, when we choose to forgive someone, this person will no longer have to be in our lives. Forgiveness does not mean we have to have a relationship with the person we are forgiving. Because my ex-husband and I had children together and we are both committed parents, we will forever be connected and in each other's company at various times for the rest of our lives.

Although my ex-husband did express that he had forgiven me, his outward behavior toward me did not mirror what he said. I will not throw my ex-husband under the bus, but I will tell you that he exhibited behavior toward me that caused me to have to turn the other cheek. Not once, twice or three times but many, many times.

I kept the olive branch extended. I chose to embrace scripture, "How many times must you forgive your brother? Seventy times seven" says the Lord (**Matthew 18:21-22**).

Never triangulate your children.

Not easy to do. My daughters were my inspiration.

Seek Forgiveness and Extend Your Love
The choice to step into vulnerability is no easy task. Courage and the willingness to put your feelings aside and risk getting hurt or rejected can be overwhelming or just plain frightening. Rebuilding relationships or strengthening relationships requires vulnerability to hear the truth someone has to share. The more you step into vulnerability the easier it becomes and you begin to see amazing growth in yourself and your relationships.

Asking for forgiveness can be just as difficult as stepping into vulnerability. Uttering requests of forgiveness takes great strength and courage. Whether we seek forgiveness or extend forgiveness, healing takes place in our hearts. An expansion of love is created moving you forward to create loving and healthy relationships.

Extending kindness when you are hurting takes courage. Putting your feelings aside is not easy, but will always move you forward to the greater good in life. Kindness is an extension of love, and when it is practiced, it will enhance and grow you as well as benefit your relationships. Be an example of extending love.

Chapter 7: Embracing a New Journey

The Power of Personal Development

"A lifestyle change begins with a vision and a single step." (Jeff Galloway)

One of the wisest decisions I have ever made in my life was to invest in myself and embark on a personal development journey. The financial and time sacrifice were worth their weight in gold.

Attending leadership conferences was time well spent and a highlight for me in my busy schedule. Meeting like-minded people from around the globe was just as exciting as it was interesting. We all had a common interest in becoming the best possible versions of ourselves as well as helping others transform their lives through the power of personal development.

One particular leadership conference I attended in Orlando, FL offered me a more than fabulous experience. The conference was four days long, and I had been hearing session after session of talented speakers on the topic of leadership for several days. During one of the sessions, I realized that I needed a break from the information overload.

I decided to take a walk and sit for a bit outside on the patio. A friend I had just met asked if she could join me. My friend approached a man sitting at a table by himself and politely asked if we could join him. With a smile on his face he replied that we were welcome to join him.

As we sat and did the informal introductions I began a conversation with the gentleman. I shared a bit of my story with him about my divorce and seeking to rebuild my life and feeling like I might never regain Leslie again.

This chance meeting was a divine appointment by God. Little did I know when I met him that he is a life coach. We decided to reconnect when the conference ended to determine if I would like to embark on life coaching sessions with him.

When we reconnected, we discussed the financial and time commitment as well as the life-changing experience I would receive if I remained committed to being open to being coached, as well as showing up and doing the work that was asked of me. It was a huge stretch for me financially. I agreed to work with him, believing it would be a life-changing experience.

He did not let me down. My life has been thrust forward in a very positive direction. Three years of once-a-week coaching has impacted my life in so many favorable ways.

My life coach has been non-judgemental, loving and kind. He has asked me questions to help me to discover and unlock pain and hurt that I did not realize I had been carrying emotionally.

My initial sessions began with my life coach asking me to go way back into my first memory as a child. I recalled an evening in the summer when I was about four years old. It was a hot summer night, the only room that was air conditioned was my parents' bedroom, my siblings and I were sleeping on the floor. I woke up to my parents fighting. I remember sitting up and asking what was wrong and was told to go back to sleep.

I grew up in a home where my mom and dad had verbal outbursts toward each other quite often. They yelled so loud that the neighbors could hear their arguments, especially in the summertime when the windows were open. The arguments included my dad cursing extensively. I felt so embarrassed and ashamed. My parents were the only parents who behaved this way in the neighborhood.

Buried within my subconscious were memories of experiences that left me feeling unworthy and shameful. Now, as an adult I am able to identify negative emotional blocks and began to change how I processed and viewed my life experiences.

The power of personal development is life-altering. It can provide the opportunity to thrust yourself forward into the realm of understanding what actions and behaviors one must embrace and one must give up to live your best life possible.

I would like to share with you one of the most impactful sessions on my life that I had with my life coach:

I had been working with my life coach for about a year and he had been helping me navigate some extremely difficult waters with my ex-husband. We had been divorced for about five years at this time, and I was filled with feelings of anger and resentment. Session after session we would discuss how

I could best move through the turbulent waters with success and he gave me some possible solutions as well as some actions to avoid.

Love and forgiveness were always at the forefront of my life coach moving me through difficult experiences with my ex-husband. I wanted to display the love of Christ in my life and that meant including my ex-husband. My extension of love could not depend on the behavior of my ex-husband towards me, good or bad.

Expectation Management would be a helpful strategy. Hurt people hurt people. My ex-husband was hurt and angry. I needed to meet my ex-husband where he was emotionally. It did not matter how I thought he should behave toward me. It was imperative for our relationship to not continue to spiral downward as a now-divorced couple. I had to take the higher road.

I needed to avoid lashing out verbally or having the mindset of "an eye for an eye".

I wanted to be set free emotionally. I wanted to run from the problems of divorce and also run from my ex-husband. During one particular session, I was standing in my bedroom leaning up against my dresser. The room was dimly lit, as my life coach and I talked about my anger toward my former husband. I was furious with my ex-husband. The Lord began to speak to my heart. As I remained sensitive to the Holy Spirit, tears began to stream down my face. My voice began to quiver as I began to say that my ex-husband is a good man.

At that moment, there was a huge sense of compassion in my heart toward the man to whom I used to be married. Honesty, vulnerability and love moved me forward to experience full and vibrant healing. Truth coupled with love were the two ingredients needed to restore my soul.

The thought that my ex is a good man would change my life forever. I was willing to pay attention to the Lord's leading. I stepped out in the position of being vulnerable with my life coach. I spoke what God sees in my ex-husband. I chose to understand my ex through embracing the power of compassion and empathy.

I extended unconditional love despite my feelings. My heart was thrust forward in healing.

Although my marriage is over, I desire to move forward looking at the good character traits in my ex-husband.

With the help of my life coach, I adopted strategies to purge unhealthy thought patterns that did not serve me well. At times I found myself pondering experiences of the past relating to my marriage or another area of my life that brought up feelings of sorrow, regret or failure. I would recall to memory the scripture verses that wrote of God's love for me as well as HIS restorative power.

My past does not determine my future. New opportunities were beginning to emerge.

Excelling in My New Sales Gig
My professional sales career began to blossom. I had been sought out for hire by the owner of a successful local company. I entered into an industry I had absolutely no knowledge or experience in selling their products.

I was excited to embark on yet another employment opportunity that would increase my sales skills and provide an opportunity for increasing my annual salary. Taking on the challenge to enter an industry I knew nothing about was not easy. There were countless hours of training to prepare me to begin to sell on the showroom floor.

I have to give kudos to my wonderful manager who was so attentive and skilled in her sales training. My co-workers were also willing to help me succeed by answering all sorts of technical and computer operations questions on the spot. My heart will be forever grateful.

Commitment to my personal development journey coupled with hiring a life coach helped to prepare me to excel in my new sales position. With no past experience selling appliances, within the first full year selling on the showroom floor, I finished second in my showroom writing $1.4 million dollars in sales. My second full year on the sales floor is projected to exceed $1.7 million in sales. My income is climbing and success is mine to claim.

Beginning to Thrive
Year after year after year of unceasing prayer and hard work to thrust myself forward was beginning to pay off. Often I would repeat to myself, "do not grow weary while doing good" (**Galatians 6:9**).

Emotional and physical healing were taking root. I was beginning to embark on short travel excursions with family and friends. Life was gifting blessings on many fronts.

A weekend away hiking with my youngest daughter brought with it summertime fun and was a time to be cherished. We spent time catching up and talking about life and what we dreamed of for the future. We shopped, sipped coffee at a local coffee shop and hiked several 2,000-foot mountains. It was not difficult, but it did take a good bit of exercise to get to the top of the summit and experience beautiful views of the mountains.

We had dinner on the rooftop of one of the local restaurants. We laughed and enjoyed our mother-and-daughter conversation.

We celebrated the graduation from college for both of my daughters. Knowing I had laid a strong foundation for their education as their homeschooling mom was beyond heart-warming to me. It was a moment of great accomplishment for me as well. I poured my heart and soul into developing the perfect curriculum, coupled with extra-curricular activities to offer the best K-12 academic education for my daughters and prepare them to excel in college and life. I truly hoped to instill the love of learning in them.

God was good in giving me the strength and perseverance to get through the 15-year journey of homeschooling. My heart beamed with parental pride and joy as I watched my daughters each at their own graduation ceremony walk across the stage. Graduate school would be the next step.

Physically, I was gaining my strength, as I had gone back to the gym. As a former competitive swimmer, I returned to my love of swimming laps in the pool several times per week. I was beginning to regain myself, standing in my strength.

As a licensed esthetician, I have a passion to help people take care of their skin and look their best. I embarked on continuing to treat clients in my esthetics business and enjoying the special business relationships I had developed with my female clients. My income was exploding on all fronts.

I am forever grateful for the encouragement my clients gave me as they watched me strive to put my life back together after my divorce.

Celebrations would continue. Within five days of each other, my youngest daughter would graduate from graduate school and my oldest daughter would get married.

My daughter strove for her master's degree in accounting with perseverance and tenacity. She became a CPA at the ripe age of 22. As I watched her walk across the stage to receive her diploma, I shouted a big congratulations for all to hear!!!

I frequently prayed for her strength and endurance as she applied herself with the utmost dedication to her studies and extracurricular academic activities. She landed a CPA position with one of the most sought-after international CPA firms. Yes, I am a proud mama!!

Four days later, we celebrated a beautiful wedding on the oceanfront in Newport, RI with family and friends. I gained a fabulous son in-law. My daughter looked beautiful in the Pavonia wedding gown I was so privileged to purchase for her. My increased income came at a perfect time. My son-in-law looked as handsome as ever. Every detail was beautifully appointed.

The wedding day of your son or daughter, is an extremely special celebration. I will hold in my heart many special moments leading up to this day that I celebrated with both my daughters as we prepared for the wedding. But, my most cherished moment with my oldest daughter on her wedding day was when we were both in our gowns ready to leave for the limo ride. I took her hands, looked into her eyes and realized the moment had arrived where she grew into an amazing beautiful young woman with both heart and soul. It was my time to speak words of encouragement from mother to daughter, wishing her well and letting her go to embark on her journey with her soon-to-be husband.

I shed tears of joy.

Standing tall and confident, I felt fabulous in my gorgeous evening gown. The band was the best and we danced the night away with a packed dance floor, having the time of my life. I was determined not to let the cold behavior of my ex-husband disrupt one of the most fabulous times in my life. This evening still brings a smile to my face. I will cherish these beautiful memories with my family and friends forever.

The years of determination to train my daughters well and prepare them for life has paid off.

Life had taken a turn for the better. My dreams were becoming bigger and bigger. Faith in myself had taken root. Courage and confidence now had become my friends.

The Power of Personal Development, Goals and Habits

Transform and empower yourself through the process of personal development. Seek out the help of mentors, literature, courses and speakers who can motivate, educate and guide you through the process of personal development. The world is your oyster. Commit to a life of excellence. Claim the abundant life that is waiting for you. The power of personal development has the potential to enhance every area of your life.

Taking advantage of opportunities that abound requires a good plan of action. Goal setting and establishing healthy and productive daily habits will serve you well. Goals listed while coupled with a sequence of actions to be taken at specific periods in time will provide a roadmap for you to follow. A step by step plan of action will serve you well.

Habits performed daily with consistency have many benefits. The top five include the ability to accomplish goal after goal, being the person you most want to be, helping people around you and increasing the overall quality of your life. Start with realistic daily habits to increase your chance of successful long-term implementation.

Chapter 8: Humility Is Your Friend

Expulsion of Pride

I never thought of myself as a prideful person in the sense that I think better of myself than I do other people. However, I do have pride in myself for the many accomplishments I have achieved in life.

As I was rebuilding my life after my divorce, I found myself at a point where my financial obligations exceeded my income. There were times when my cupboards were quite bare. I would go to the supermarket and hold my breath at the cash register hoping the bill did not exceed the money I had available on my debit card. The hard reality was that sometimes I had to put a few items back on the shelf and feelings of embarrassment would fill my heart.

I was living, as they say, from hand-to-mouth.

I chose to not let my daughters or other family know the tight financial bind I was in. I was determined to work through the difficulty myself. I would tell myself that I did not want to burden my family, but I learned deep down my feelings stemmed from pride. I did not want people to know how bad my financial situation had become.

I really had gone from riches to rags. It was even possible that I could end up homeless. I had already lost two homes. I was about to lose a third.

Although I tried my hardest to make ends meet, affording my beautiful apartment in an upscale historic district by the water was becoming more and more difficult. Unfortunately, I could not see myself on the other side of financial stability.

Coming to grips with this reality, I decided that the best option for me was to move in with my mother. I sought my mom's help and asked if she would like me to keep her company and become her roommate. She gladly accepted my coming to live with her.

My mom's apartment consists of three small rooms in a retirement community complex. It is void of the many luxuries I was accustomed to living with. There is no central air, dishwasher or jetted tub. It is a tastefully-decorated humble abode filled with a mother's love.

I sold off most of my furniture for pennies on the dollar, excluding my bedroom set. I gave away many items of my clothing so I could squeeze into the living space that I would have. It was still a tight fit, but I made due with the room I was given.

My bedroom was my space to relax and spend time alone, so I made it as comfortable as possible and filled it with special pictures of my daughters and other memorabilia that brought comfort to my heart. I had found a place of refuge.

There are times I drive up the long driveway, through the parking lot of the apartment complex and would shake my head thinking that I never thought I would live in a low-income retirement housing community. It was an opportunity for me to evaluate the attitude of my heart.

Sitting on my bed and putting the finishing touches on writing this book, I heard a knock at the door. It was a sweet neighbor of ours. She handed me a piece of paper that was notifying the residents that arrangements had been made for us to receive a free box filled with food once a week for the next six months to relieve the financial burden due to the Coronavirus.

As I read the paper, I thought about how fabulous of an idea it was. Although my mom and I did not "need" the free groceries to put food on our table, I quickly prepared to make my way down to the community room where we could pick up our free groceries and a gallon of milk.

As I entered the community room, I was greeted by the maintenance manager and the property manager. They were excited to provide the gifts.

We made great use of the free groceries and had fewer trips to the grocery store. Gratitude filled my heart.

A penny saved is a penny earned.

Looking back upon the situation, I feel it was an opportunity for me to either accept the gift before me with humility or reject the offer with pride. I am glad I chose the path of humility.

"Take My yoke upon you, and learn from Me, for I am gentle and humble in heart; and you SHALL FIND REST FOR YOUR SOULS." (**Matthew 11:29**)

Appreciating God's Gifts
Moving in with my mom would prove itself to be a gift from God. We spend time together watching our favorite movies, chatting, reminiscing and encouraging each other as single women.

My mom is one of my biggest cheerleaders. In the mornings, when I leave for work she always wishes me luck in my job as I'm heading out the door. A mother's touch and love is a true blessing. I would return home at the end of the day sharing with her my wins and my total of closed sales.

Watching our favorite old-time TV shows brought us much laughter as we remembered the good old days. We would talk about how life has changed and the challenges we have overcome. We were thankful for celebrating the life God has given us. Waking up daily is a blessing.

We both were beyond thankful for living together. We felt it was a second chance for both of us to make more beautiful memories. We were both older and wiser and it was a time for me to help out my aging mother. I made sure the food shopping was done weekly, clothing was sent out to be laundered and we both contributed to taking turns cooking meals.

My mom is a great source of encouragement, and my heart is beyond grateful for her love and support as I tenaciously worked to get myself back on my feet.

I made friends in the apartment complex. I feel blessed to have been given the opportunity to encourage people who found themselves less fortunate than I was, and I like lending an ear to them when life is hitting them hard.

One morning as I walked the pathway around the building, one of the male tenants stopped me as I passed by his apartment. He was crying because his wife had just passed away in their apartment moments before. They had been married for over 50 years, and he was her caregiver up until her passing. It broke my heart, and I felt privileged to have the opportunity to listen to him and have a moment to say a prayer of peace and strength with him, as he would now be living alone.

Some people are not fortunate enough to have loved ones to grow old with. One man who lived in the retirement complex and occupied the apartment directly upstairs from my apartment, lived the last few years of his life alone. Family members did not come to visit and he had very few friends. At the age of 92, he was found dead in his apartment, and it was not discovered until several days later.

It broke my heart and brought to the forefront of my mind one of life's great lessons. Friends and family are a blessing in our lives. Keeping our relationships healthy and loving is even more important as we grow old.

It gave me an opportunity to see that my life might have other challenges, but I was spared the pain that others found themselves enduring at a much deeper level. I have options and time to rebuild myself. Others are not so fortunate.

I was reminded that we all grow old, so we should make the most of our time. Squelch the fear that can sometimes hold us back and go for the life we want to live. My motto is, "Embrace life. Today matters."

Since I have been living with my mom, one of my favorite things to do has been to take long walks around the property building. I take that time to thank God for the blessing of living with my mom. Although the apartment building in which we reside is a far cry from the beauty of my custom-built home with a heated swimming pool, I am deeply grateful for this wonderfly special time to live with my mom. We are making beautiful memories together that I will cherish for a lifetime.

The memories I make today are the moments I will look back on tomorrow!

Living a Debt-Free Life
My parents were incredibly hard-working individuals and taught me well about how to apply myself with diligence and responsibility to any and all jobs I held. Neither of my parents held a college degree. My dad was considered a blue-collar worker who held an hourly-wage position in the dairy industry.

My dad worked tirelessly to provide a home, food and clothing for our family as best as he could on the wages he earned. At times, he would hold two jobs to make ends meet. He never complained.

I hold much respect for my dad because of his strong work ethic.

When I was no more than three years old, he would take me to the dairy farm where he was responsible for hooking the cows up to the machines to be mechanically milked. Looking at the cows as they passed by me one by one absolutely frightened me. Their eyes seemed so big and oversized.

Frightened, I would retreat into my mother's arms for safety. I didn't realize then that the cows were harmless.

I hold fond memories in my heart of the days my dad would take me to jobs where he would fill vats with all the ingredients to make ice cream. I remember the vats being huge and turning out hundreds of gallons of ice cream.

Yes, I did get to sample some of the finished products.

For most of my early childhood years, my mom was a stay-at-home mom. When she did enter the workforce, she took jobs that paid minimum wage. Needless to say, I did not grow up in an affluent home where the financial stewardship of saving and investing money was taught.

My family existed on the week-to-week paycheck schedule. Thankfully, my parents were not the type to accumulate large amounts of debt. Credit cards were only used for the necessities in life.

When I was engaged to my ex-husband, I had a $6,000 debt from college. Before I got married, I paid my student loans off in full.

During the twenty-three years I was married, we never accumulated debt. We lived according to our financial means. We purchased luxurious items only when we earned bonuses or our annual income had increased.

When I found myself in the position of being divorced and having antiquated employment skills to enter the workforce, my earning rate started at minimum wage. It took years for me to increase my earning potential. During this time, financial hardship began to take root leading to an accumulation of debt.

It was just not possible for me to keep up with all the financial responsibilities as a single mom. It did not take long for me to draw on all the funds that were available through my 401K plan and money from my divorce settlement that I had put in the bank.

I was also left with high medical bills of about $20,000 due to some compromised physical health issues I experienced, which added insult to injury.

Before I knew it, I was drowning in debt, and the burden was very heavy.

I was desperate to change my situation. I chose to not file for bankruptcy. Instead, I sought the advice of a financial agency that could help to settle a portion of my debt and pay the remaining balance in payments over time.

The monthly payment I had to make to clear up my debt was not easy. Although it offered a pathway to becoming debt-free, I still was burdened financially,

Within a few years of making the required monthly payments, I became debt-free. I gave a big sigh of relief and vowed I would never accumulate debt again.

I live debt-free today. It is a freeing and liberating experience. No longer am I in bondage to financial institutions making monthly payments that burden me emotionally and financially.

I live in freedom and abundance. It is absolutely wonderful. I am continuing to train myself to keep purchases simple and to live on a budget that continues to allow me freedom from the burden of debt.

My car is paid in full. I buy clothes and amenities with cash. I have learned to say "NO" to purchases that will put me in the position of financial stress. I continue to seek ways to increase my financial abundance and stability.

I have embraced a simplified debt-free life, and I am loving every minute of it!!!

Live Gratefully, Humbly and Debt-Free
Expunging pride from your heart is essential to move forward to experience a life of abundance. Take time to reflect and evaluate if you have a pride-filled or humble heart. Humility is your friend while pride is your foe. Humility allows you to experience the ability to receive with a thankful heart. Pride causes you to judge and reject precious acts of kindness extended toward you. Choose humility and reap the good gifts that are sent your way.

Having an attitude of gratitude will serve you well. Start a gratitude journal listing daily just one or two (more if you would like) things you are grateful for. Keeping a list will help you to keep track of all the abundance you have in your life. Focus on the good.

The benefits of debt-free living are plentiful. Freedom from debtors releases stress. Freedom from debt opens up a wide variety of financial options, saving and investing are just two. Make a plan to become debt-free. The process may not happen overnight. Have a stick-to-it attitude and in time you will be debt free.

Chapter 9:
Living Your Best Life

Self-Image

My journey of self-discovery has been an up and down experience as well as a twisting and turning road. It is a journey I am glad I have embraced.

I have been studying the topic of self-image through the teachings of Empowerment Mentoring offered by Paul Martinelli and Roddy Gailbriath in conjunction with Dr. Harold Bafitis. Dr. Bafitis is a renowned plastic surgeon.

I have found Dr. Bafitis's knowledge is valuable as I have set out to increase my self-esteem. I would like to share with you his expertise regarding the topic of self-image:

According to Dr. Bafitis "The inner image we hold of ourselves is a powerful force in our lives. These ideas of the sort of people we are, of how successful we are supposed to be of how we are meant to think and feel and act in response to our life experiences can be collectively and conceptually labeled as the self-image.

It is interesting to consider that we are not born with these ideas about ourselves. In fact, we are not born with any ideas at all. Where do these ideas come from, then? They come from experiences of our lives and from our perception of those experiences.

Our experiences are stored away as an "understanding" of the world to help us with future experiences. These personal "conclusions", or beliefs, often formed unconsciously, are shaped from our positive experiences as well as our negative experiences. Those experiences are sometimes dreadful, sometimes wonderful, sometimes dull as a doornail.

The more intense the emotions associated with the experience, the more "important" we unconsciously deem those experiences to be. As a consequence of this, the beliefs are "filled" with more importance.

These experiences are typically, but not solely, accumulated during the early part of our life and often, not just from our own experiences, but from the comments, actions and responses of other people.

Self-image is ideas about us that are placed in our minds by other people, without us realizing it, before we had the ability to think for ourselves.

Because the beliefs are stored in our subconscious mind, tucked away below the level of consciousness, we are often not even aware that they are there at all, let alone have cause to question their validity or helpfulness."

We are shaped by our experiences.

When I think about the earlier years of my life and what experiences impacted me contributing to a low self-image, I think of two impactful events.

The first happened when I was in second grade. I was late for school one day because my mom misplaced her car keys. By the time she found them and drove me to school, class had already begun.

I entered into my class to find there was a spelling bee taking place. The room was divided into two teams, each standing on opposite sides of the room facing each other. I quickly stepped into the coat room to hang up my winter coat. While I was in the coat room my teacher asked me why I was late and I explained that my mom lost her car keys so we were late heading out to school.

The class burst into laughter, and it felt like they were laughing at me. I was embarrassed and became emotionally stressed. As I took my position on my team, my teacher immediately called on me to spell the word "fix."

I remember like it was yesterday. I spelled it as "fic". It was such an easy word to spell, and I blew it. I walked back to my seat, sat down and felt completely embarrassed and humiliated.

The second event that played a huge role in my feelings of not being enough happened when I was 14 years old.

I was a competitive swimmer and always trained to compete for the 100-yard freestyle race. One day, my coach needed me to fill a spot swimming the 100-yard butterfly in an older age group. I was going to have to swim against three of the most skilled and swift butterfly stroke athletes who were known for achieving fast times.

The butterfly stroke is the most difficult stroke to master. It takes great strength and endurance to swim 100 yards successfully and to completion. Knowing there was no way for me to get out of the race, I took my position on the starting block. When the gun went off to begin the race, I dove into the water and swam to the best of my ability.

By the time I reached the 45-yard mark, I was exhausted. My arms could barely complete a full stroke. I was void of the necessary strength to continue. I decided I would climb out of the pool and pulled myself onto the pool deck with whatever strength I had left. I felt like a failure. My team needed me to finish the race to get the one point needed to contribute to the score to beat our competition and win the meet.

Feeling defeated, I burst into tears as I walked by the hundreds of viewers to take my seat on the bleachers.

This experience was devastating and left me with a poor self-image. Thoughts of my not being enough plagued my mind. I was not enough to be successful; I was not enough to live the life of my dreams.

> "Until you make the unconscious conscious, it will rule your life and you will call it fate" - Carl Jung

During one particular session with my life coach, he took me through an exercise to help me discover God's special name for me. I discovered God's unique name for me is His "Special Lady." I have laid claim to this name, and it has helped to thrust me forward believing God has planned and wants the best for me.

His "Special Lady" has been given unique gifts and talents to be shared with the world.

Looking back at these events in my life, I could now understand how my emotions planted feelings of self-doubt. Becoming aware, I needed to make the unconscious conscious. I could move from self-doubt to self-confidence.

I had told myself lies about myself, and I had believed them.

I am enough and have always been enough. In fact, I am beyond enough. I am His "Special Lady."

Squelching Fear

> "Everything you want is on the other side of fear"
> - Jack Canfield

My desire to move forward in life and take on new challenges met up with the ugly head of fear.

Thankfully, because of my personal development training, I did not submit or surrender to fear. I recognized that it existed, and it brought to mind a few principles I had been taught through reading one of my favorite leadership books by John C. Maxwell, "Failing Forward."

There are many great teaching points mentioned in the book to move one beyond the fear of failure. One of the points that Maxwell makes in his book that I keep at the forefront of my mind is, "There is no achievement without failure." One must be willing to take a chance and risk failure to achieve success.

Getting out of my comfort zone and stepping into my growth zone has allowed me to excel in life. Recalling past experiences of success moved me beyond being overwhelmed and filled with doubt. Once again, I went forward and took a step of faith. Success was mine for the taking.

Years ago, I joined a local aerobics studio. It wasn't long before the owner of the studio asked me if I would be interested in becoming an aerobics instructor. I was excited and thankful for such an invitation, but fear gripped my mind with the thought of actually instructing a class.

I accepted the invitation and completed all the necessary training requirements with flying colors. It was not long until I was ready to instruct a class on my own. The first time I was to take front and center stage with the class, I was beyond fearful.

I drove to the studio from my home playing classical music to help calm my nerves. When I arrived at the studio, I remember heading straight to the ladies room to practice deep-breathing exercises right before the class began.

The time came when class had to start, I took my position as instructor with a class of 40 experienced students and began instructing the class. I completed the class, however not with perfect instruction. The good news is that within a few months of instructing, I was comfortable teaching and earned the position as one of the best instructors in the studio.

This was one of my biggest accomplishments in my early-adult life, and it paved a pathway for me to have the courage to take on bigger and more difficult tasks. I had a goal that was worthy of failing at because I knew that when I succeeded at it, it would give me the strength to power myself forward.

Not only was I successful in overcoming my fear, but the position as an aerobics instructor would provide me with the opportunity to make great connections in the business community. One of my students helped me to land an excellent sales position with a Fortune 500 company selling local area networks. I received extensive sales training and have implemented the information throughout my sales profession.

Stepping Up and Out

I start every day with either a prayer or reading a passage from one of my favorite books.

This passage touches my heart, as it gives me strength to go out and live my best life.

My Princess
Give Me Your Plans

I know you have an idea in your head on how everything should unfold in your life. Even today you have an agenda. Because I love you, I need you to give Me back all your plans for today and for all your tomorrows. If you let Me have your day I can then intervene with something special. My intervention will give you more joy in your journey than your good intentions. I know all that your heart longs for, and I want to do more for you than you could ever do for yourself. So, give Me a chance to change your agenda from ordinary to extraordinary, because that's the kind of life I've destined you to live, My beloved.

Love,
Your King and your Planner

"Commit to the Lord whatever you do and your plans will succeed."
- (**Proverbs 16:3**, NIV)

Venturing out to live my best life would entail embracing the courage to take one step at a time. Each new step would be taken on the firm foundation of the "wins" I was now beginning to experience.

Dreaming big dreams was no longer pie-in-the-sky thinking.

I learned a valuable lesson from one of my former mentors while working in the hotel industry. My mentor modeled for me what it looks like to embrace new responsibilities and projects. He encouraged me to step into courage and say "YES" to the project when you are asked to do something you do not know how to do. You can figure out how to get it done later.

This lesson has played a valuable role in my success as I take steps and go forward in life.

Because I said "yes" to investing in myself and embarking on the journey of personal development, I have had the opportunity to meet and be mentored by talented and successful people. They model for me professional as well as personal achievement, excelling beyond the average.

Success requires action. We can dream and practice the best mindset training but unless we commit to action steps we will remain in nothing but a hopeful and dream like state.

I can thank my business coach for his brilliant expertise in this area. Because I was committed to growth coupled with a strong desire to achieve my dreams, I embraced the principles my business coach taught me for business building and success. Applying the principles and strategies he taught have helped me to have a roadmap to follow for business development and success.

I am grateful for the constructive encouragement and accountability I received from my business coach. His training is not for the wishy-washy, show-up-when-you-want-to, do-the-work-when-you-have-time type of people. Commitment and dedication are behaviors that are required for success in all areas of our lives.

We get in life what we give to life. When we commit to giving all we have in our mind, body and soul we increase our chances to achieve the biggest dreams of our life.

A life lived with excellence is not for the weak or faint of heart.

We must run the race of life set before us with a steadfast tenacious spirit to achieving our goals. Winning is the only option. Expectation of encountering challenges and obstacles should not take us by surprise or deter us from going forward to live our best life. Embrace the attitude that what you go through will grow you!!

"Do you not know that those who run in a race all run, but only one receives the prize? Run in such a way as you may win" (**1 Corinthians 9:24**)

Living our lives by sowing the seed of our gifts and talents will certainly in time bring forth a harvest of reaping rewards in our own lives and the lives of those around us. Let us go forward with strength and determination.

Living Your Best Life
Today, my life looks extremely different than the day I walked out of the courthouse as a newly-divorced woman. All areas of my life have blossomed and joy fills my heart.

I stepped into courage and strength. I took risks. I became vulnerable and borrowed the belief others had in me until I believed in myself. By doing so, I am now reaping a tremendous amount of blessings in my life.

I have gone from having over $50,000 fifty of debt accumulated to living debt-free. My annual income has increased an additional $50,000, and the increase will continue. Investing in yourself pays off. Four years of working with my life coach has paid high dividends in all areas of my life way beyond my financial success.

I have uprooted shame, blame, guilt, regret and low self-esteem. I now walk with peace, joy, confidence, strong self-esteem and high regard for myself. Courage and confidence are my friends and walk with me daily.

My sales career is booming. I entered into the appliance sales industry three years ago with no knowledge of appliance sales and three years later my sales have exceeded $1.5 million annually and is growing. I work with the most talented and successful appliance sales reps with decades of experience. I now hold a spot as one of the top-ranking sales reps in the company.

I embraced the opportunity to hire a business coach to help me strategize and implement a business plan for establishing my life coaching business. By doing so, I now have a thriving life coaching business, a podcast show and will have published my first book. Fruits of my labor are being produced.

Through my leadership development associations and church activities, new friends abound from all parts of the world. I am truly blessed to have so many friends. Invitations are plentiful for me to visit their homelands and reconnect.

Looking for a new home is now in the works, and it is so exciting to think about having a place of my own where I can entertain family and friends celebrating life together and making fabulous memories. Designing the color scheme, purchasing new furnishings, setting up my kitchen with all new dinnerware and designing a new home office is a dream coming true.

Living with my mom has been a blessing beyond measure. We have had the opportunity to love and support each other. We have helped each other build a new bridge to the next chapter in our lives. A breath of new life has filled each of our lives and I will cherish forever the new memories my mom and I have the opportunity to make.

I have forgiven my ex-husband and hold respect for him as a devoted and dedicated father to our daughters.

Most importantly, my relationship with my now-young-adult daughters continues to thrive. Our relationship is based on a deep respect and love for one another. Through the years they have watched me display attributes that bring healing, forgiveness, trust, commitment and love to the place of brokenness. I am forever grateful for their support and encouragement. We cheer each other on to pursue life to its fullest. They will always be the wind beneath my wings. My beautiful daughters, who I love to the moon and back.

"God will restore what the locust have eaten" - (**Joel 2:25**)

Build Your Self-Esteem

Self-esteem or your image you hold of yourself will affect every area of your life. If your self-esteem is keeping you from experiencing life's best, you can do something about it. The good news is, your self-esteem can be improved. Hiring a life coach to help you develop a plan of action to increase your self-esteem that you can be proud of is a wise financial and time investment.

As you seek to take on new challenges in life, fear can become a roadblock. Reviewing past successes can give you courage to squelch fear and take on a new challenge. Life coaching can also be a helpful resource in this area as well. Having a coaching partner to walk beside you and give you support, encouragement and to hold you accountable is worth its weight in gold.

Saying "yes" to new opportunities that are presented to you will set you forward to growth. Each new experience in life has something to teach us if we maintain a teachable mindset. The more we welcome and join in on new adventures the more we have the opportunity to grow. Growth allowing favorable experiences will provide the opportunity to increase self-esteem.

Taking one step at a time to reach your goals will serve you well.

Conclusion:
I hold a value in my life that Jesus Christ will be the foundation of my dreams and plans. I have committed to seeking His wisdom and blessings for all the actions and steps I take in my life.

As I put one foot in front of the other to move forward in my life, holding to this mindset has served me well.

My Prayer for YOU

I pray you choose to be set free from the shame and blame game and embrace the unconditional love of God. I pray you intentionally and with love let go of the past. I pray you acknowledge the loving conviction of the Lord through the power of the Holy Spirit in your life and act to make changes where necessary.

I pray for you to forgive those who persecute you, as the Lord has forgiven us in our transgressions. I pray you take the high road in life, extending the olive branch when necessary and for as long as necessary. I pray you choose the path of Love securing sustaining joy and peace in your heart.

I pray you make a commitment to yourself to live expressing the gifts and talents uniquely appointed to you by God. I pray you will choose to share your talents and gifts with the world.

I pray for prosperity to abound in all areas of your life. I pray the wind will always be at your back.

In Thee, O Lord, I have taken refuge: Let me never be ashamed. (**Psalm 71:1**)

Blessings to you!!

Reference Page

Empowerment Mentoring. 2018. "Ride The Fear To The Life Of Your Dreams". By Paul Martinelli and Roddy Gailbraith. Guide Book Page 1.

Empowerment Mentoring. 2018. "Self-Image Mastery". By Paul Martinelli and Roddy Gailbraith. Program Action Guide. Page 16-18.

Free, T. (2020, October 29). Five Benefits of Developing The Right Habits. Retrieved November 30, 2020, from https://www.productiveandfree.com/blog

Maxwell, J. C. (2000). *Failing Forward: How To Make The Most Of Your Mistakes.* Thomas Nelson.

Ryrie, C. C. (1978). *Ryrie Study Bible: New Testament: New American standard version.* Chicago, Illinois: Moody Press.

Shepherd, S. R. (2004). *His princess: Love letters from your king* (pp. 96-97). Sisters, OR: Multnomah.

I Would Love to Hear From You

To write Leslie Sepe personally, or to book Leslie to speak at your church or event, please email:

leslie@lesliesepeconsulting.com

If you would like to join her Facebook group (for women only):

Courageous Confidence: Ignite Your Power and Potential

Thank you

Made in the USA
Coppell, TX
16 June 2021